My First Korean
Alphabets

Picture Book with English Translations

Published By: MyFirstPictureBook.com

ㄱ

고양이

Cat

ㄴ

나무

Tree

ㄷ

도끼

Axe

ㄹ

라디오

Radio

ㅁ

무지개

Rainbow

ㅂ

바나나

Banana

ㅅ

사과

Apple

ㅇ

오리

Duck

ㅈ

자동차

Car

ㅊ

초콜릿

Chocolate

ㅋ

코끼리

Elephant

ㅌ

토마토

Tomato

ㅍ

포도

Grape

ㅎ

하늘

Sky

ㅏ

바퀴

Wheel

ㅑ

양파

Onion

ㅓ

거울

Mirror

ㅕ

여우

Fox

ㅗ

오리

Duck

ㅛ

요구르트

Yogurt

ㅜ

우산

Umbrella

ㄲ

유리

Glass

一

트럭

Truck (Lorry)

1

시계

Clock